ONE
IS CANADA

Maxine Trottier

Illustrated by
Bill Slavin

HarperCollins*PublishersLtd*

1 One is Canada.

Two are the hands joining in friendship. So many people have made this their home.

One is Canada.

3

Three are the oceans,
full of life. Salty and deep,
they wash our shores.
Two is for friendship, the joining of hands.
One is Canada.

ARCTIC

ATLANTIC

PACIFIC

4

Four are the compass points from Nunavut to Pelee, sunrise to sunset, north, south, east, west.
Three are the oceans, washing the land.
Two is for friendship and one is Canada.

NUN

Five are the Great Lakes, fresh-water jewels. Those who brave them sail our south shore.
Four is the compass, north, south, east, west.
Three are the oceans and two is for friendship.
One is Canada.

6

Six are the Six Nations and all the First People. Like the sky and the wind they are one with the land.
Five are the Great Lakes, fresh-water jewels.
Four is the compass; three the oceans.
Two is for friendship and one is Canada.

7

Seven is the Group of Seven, dreamers and painters. They made Canada a work of art.
Six are the Six Nations and all the First People,
Five the Great Lakes and four the compass.
Three are the oceans and two is for friendship.
One is Canada.

Eight are the lines we proudly sing. *O Canada!* the sound of our voices strong and free.
Seven is the Group of Seven, dreamers and painters,
Six the First People and five the Great Lakes.
Four is the compass and three are the oceans.
Two is for friendship and one is Canada.

9
Nine are the centuries —
nine and more — since
sailors came here from afar.
Eight is for singing, *O Canada!*
Seven the dreamers and six the First People.
Five are the Great Lakes, four is the compass.
Three the oceans and two is friendship.
One is Canada.

Ten are the provinces that joined one by one. They linked their arms to build our land.

Nine is for more than nine centuries ago. Sailors stopped and saw a new world.

Eight is for singing, *O Canada!*

Seven the Group of Seven, dreamers and painters.

Six the Six Nations and all the First People.

Five the Great Lakes, our jewels of fresh water.

Four is the compass, north, south, east, west, Canada stretching in every direction.

Three are the oceans, full of life.

Two are the hands joining in friendship.

One is Canada.

One is Canada.

NOTES ON CANADA

Each of the ten illustrations in *One Is Canada* is filled with information about this country. You can find out more about Canada at http://canada.gc.ca/

 **1** Canada has been a country since Confederation Day, July 1, 1867. Most of us can only appreciate it from the ground, but several Canadian astronauts have had a chance to see Canada from outer space on the space shuttle. Canada is a nation with a rich past and an exciting future for the children who live here.

2 Canada is like a wonderful quilt made up of people from cultures around the world. There are two official languages, English and French. However, Canadians speak many other languages to each other as well. Canada is a place where all people have the chance to celebrate their ethnic origins as well as their differences. Living together in friendship, we all share Canada.

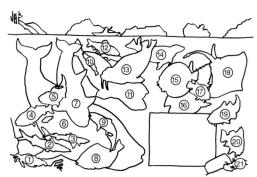 **3** Canada has one of the longest coastlines in the world: 250,000 kilometres long. Its oceans are filled with fish and wildlife of every description. From the beginning, Canadians have turned to the sea for both work and play. Preserving Canada's resources is an important goal, so that the clean water, fish and animals will always be there for everyone to enjoy.

Pacific: (1) crab (2) pacific barracuda (3) spurdog (4) sea bass and young (5) california yellowtail (6) blue whale (7) killer whale (8) pacific halibut (9) sockeye salmon

Arctic: (10) pacific hake (11) bowhead whale (12) arctic char (13) walrus (14) harp seal

Atlantic: (15) turbot (16) bluefin tuna (17) cunner (18) barndoor skate (19) cod (20) black drum (21) lobster

4 Canada is enormous! It covers almost 10,000,000 square kilometres of forests, prairies, mountains, tundra and farmland. It is a country where some things change and others stay the same. Recently, the new northern territory of Nunavut was created. To the south, Monarch butterflies stop each fall at Point Pelee as they have for countless years. Canadians look forward as well as back.

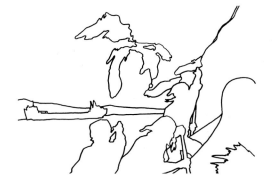 **5** The Great Lakes hold almost 20% of the world's fresh water. Commercial ships and pleasure boats navigate them. Long ago the *coureurs des bois* paddled the lakes in large canoes carrying the furs with which they traded. Today between 50 million and 100 million metric tonnes of goods pass through the Great Lakes on freighters each year.

6 There are more than 600 bands of First People living in Canada. This illustration shows only a few. Their customs are varied, and the more than 50 languages they speak are all different. Yet First People everywhere in Canada share a closeness to the land that was once theirs alone. The cultures and traditions that they keep alive show respect for all living things and people.

(1) Inuit iglu (2) Inuit family (3) Tlingit Sun and Raven totem pole (4) Tlingit chief's (or noble's) house (5) Nootka man wearing twined basketry hat (6) Kwakiutl chief (or noble) wearing a button blanket (7) Salish woman with child (8) Haida man holding copper shield (9) Blood ceremonial lodge (10) Blackfoot man in buffalo robe (11) Blackfoot chief holding pipe (12) Young Cree woman (13) Cree elder (14) Oneida longhouse (15) Wyandot youth (16) Chippewa child (17) Chippewa woman (18) Iroquois man holding two row wampum

7 Canada has given the world wonderful music, books and art. The artists who called themselves the Group of Seven created a Canadian style of painting. They travelled the North, sketching and painting in the wilds. The work they did was both bold and fresh. It changed art in this country, and gave other artists the freedom to show Canada as they saw it.

The Group of Seven: (1) A.Y. Jackson (2) F.H. Varley (3) Lawren Harris (4) Arthur Lismer (5) J.E.H. MacDonald (6) Franklin H. Carmichael (7) Frank H. Johnston

8 *O Canada* is Canada's national anthem. There have been a number of versions since it was composed in 1880 by Calixa Lavallée. The version we sing today was proclaimed on July 1, 1980, in a public ceremony on Parliament Hill in Ottawa. Our national anthem has eight sentences in its first verse. The first sentence, "O Canada!," has eight characters.

9 Almost 1,000 years ago the Norse came to Canada in Viking ships. The remains of their settlement were discovered in 1960 at L'Anse aux Meadows, Newfoundand. No one knows how long the Norse stayed, but they did build workshops, houses and a forge. Pieces of jewellery and part of a spindle were uncovered; this tells us that women lived there as well as men.

10 Canada has ten provinces: British Columbia, Alberta, Saskatchewan, Manitoba, Ontario, Quebec, New Brunswick, Nova Scotia, Prince Edward Island and Newfoundland, which includes Labrador. It has three territories: the Northwest Territories, Nunavut and the Yukon. Each province and territory has its own capital; the capital of Canada is Ottawa. We are one Canada, united by the red maple leaf flag that flies over us all.

for every child in Canada
— *Maxine Trottier*

to Dawson
— *Bill Slavin*

HarperCollins Publishers Ltd
Suite 2900, Hazelton Lanes, 55 Avenue Road
Toronto, Canada M5R 3L2.

ONE IS CANADA
Text copyright © 1999 by Maxine Trottier.
Illustrations copyright © 1999 by Bill Slavin.
All rights reserved.

For information address
http://www.harpercanada.com
Printed in Hong Kong

99 00 01 02 03 First edition 10 9 8 7 6 5 4 3 2 1

Canadian Cataloguing in Publication Data

Trottier, Maxine,
One is Canada

ISBN 0-00-224556-6 (bound)

1. Canada — Juvenile poetry.
2. Counting — Juvenile poetry.
I. Slavin, Bill.
II. Title.

PS9589.R685O53 1999   jC811'.54   C98-932586-5   PR9199.3.T76O53 1999